FLAMING HEARTBEATS

POEMS

FLAMING HEARTBEATS

POEMS

Gift Foraine Amukoyo

Soft Grid Limited

Gift Foraine Amukoyo

Published by

Soft Grid Limited

Plot 6, Block 23, Satellite Town

Calabar, Cross River, Nigeria

+234 (0)8027676550, +234 (0)8053110637

E-mail: softgridbooks@gmail.com

softgridltd@hotmail.com

www.softgridbookslimited.com

© Gift Foraine Amukoyo

First Published in 2018

ISBN 978-978-56095-0-9

Soft Grid Books

First Printing, October 2018

Dedication

To people, beautiful and compassionate at heart

Songs of the Heart

Sky Rage

On every strike it bellows
The sky comes stiffer to plunder
There is a storm to withstand
Whether it brews thunder
Or flickers lightening fair

The rain will not wither
Until it feeds the earth with its seeds
It is its desire to pelt with socks or sucks
Since the soil is not shy of its thrusts
Your seal is to shove or shelve it floods

On flicker
My heart pit-a-pat for you
All I crave is to part your bosom
And feather kisses to your heart
To wet your soul and body
And put your beats on flipper
To warm my cold with your fire
For this warmth you give to me
Has left this throbbing softness

Silent Embers

Once sparky crispy and fly
These embers have gone silent
Now dumb and deaf to my soles
Lonelier than the sober break of dawn
As cold as if,
This hearth never bore warmth
Lighters are lulled to sleep
Clouds are impatient
Like the feet of a hurricane
When the half moon
Kisses stars slowly adieu
The peaky moon moos on the night more
And it feels not lonely
What wholly had it known itself
To love itself
To feel itself
I awaited the hose in me
But the pipes so offish
Pipes piping sundry tunes
From myself, so I search
Marching the hides of hades
Sitting on this ceiling
The will wheels and reels
To let go; so I let go

Bat Love

Love me if you want
I cannot beg for it
Touch me if you desire
It can make broken passions mend
I open up to your caresses
For the feel of your hands
Shivers down my spine
My insides melt like wax

Your careless whispers
Wire butterflies up my nerves
The tingling on my nipples
Makes my vulva diary product

Your sword plunges my sheath
With furious intake of breath
And always the weakling surrenders
With reckless abandon
Swearing on wild oaths never to succumb again

Yet, every time you rattle,
I flourish like a blooming flower
And come to you like a drenched lamb
In need of warm hearth

How can I still crave your every touch
When my love is ground to dust?
Why will I not sail from this unrequited love?
Am I a prisoner of my own desire?

Your making love speaks loud truth
Your hearty love tells lies upon lies

And the caring a sham
I love you, but

I break loose from here
To find and love me
Care and find worth for myself
And so, free will I be

Shape of the Heart

The L.O.V.E alphabetical letters
So seems the best figure
Reserved the spelling of the word love
Cherished and adored
Is he or she that coined it
It's so right and befitting
I want to believe
With sordid conviction
The person was a seasoned artist
Mastered with gifted insights
Talented with great painting brush
Tailing in beautiful captivation of purity
Viewing heart-warming images

The heart's shape symbolizes love
Loving has to do with the heart
Two, four, six hearts
Merged in mutual similitude
Pulsing to a uniting goal
The heart is a tissue of blood
Pumping blood to every sect
Of the living body
Breathing in life to every cell
Fuelling the body to duel with emotions
Is love blood?

Two hearts merge as one
Flow in flow of blood ties
Does every heart
Beat in the same rhythm?
Put your heart to mine
Heart to heart

Let us observe if it beats in a unit
Yeah, it's indeed going on same pulse
I can hear the
Throb! Throb!! of your heart
Same as mine
They are so freely humane
When two hearts yearn for each other
The connection is vaguely unexplainable
But it's exclusively expressible
When one heart takes off on a marathon
Only then will the gyration change
The tempo of the runner increases

One racing heart
Beats faster than the other
After a while it takes on the regular beat
It cannot be on the run for all times
It must return to the heart's rhythm
That always, grease glows the mind
Giving hues of colours to the skin
It may shut down when the mind is hurt
Or if the body is killed
It is a jewel every bosom is endowed
The shape is heartfelt and precious

Love is a gem
Beautiful gems are rare
When you find one
Cuddle it to your bosom
Love is beautiful to the beauties at heart
Love is baleful to the beasts at heart
For every sense and motion

Two organs were given
But one heart

One heart to find its matching shape
And make sweet love together
One, one in pair
Pair in pairs

Dark Teaser

A new dawn is to break loose
Night and day lay blanket naked
Arms wrapped and cuddling warmly
They would not disengage their communion in a hurry
Both limbs tangled and untangled
Caressing and cupping figures
Night noosing his nose on day's soft nape
Running his knuckles all over her light form
Teasing and mesmerizing her with cloudy kisses
He would not want to let her go
She is his shining flare
The lighter to his dark hood

Oh my knight, stop it, you must go now
He spreads over and partly covers his thighs with hers
Oh no, you must get off you randy night crawler
You must go grace the beds of your numerous mistresses
You're every lady's man, not mine to keep
Go now, you mustn't keep them waiting
They have been awake dawn to dusk
Tending their subjects, lying in wait
For your cover to lay rest and relax
In the good warmth you bear
No one can tell your mood swings
It is at times horrifying and sorrowful
Bearing nightmares or hugging the body with cold hands
I thank the heavens high above for bestowing the best moods
On you whenever you grace my chambers
You are the feared and fearless knight
Your teasing stores untold satisfaction and displeasure
Though I am jealous, I want you to take with you
This romantic mood to your next holdings

Leave me now straying knight
I need to shower my full light to the fortress
It is my stationed duty as regional forecast
And off course you must head on
To lay cover with your mistresses in other realms
It is our destiny to remain single but mingle
To be companions for restricted times
It is the lot we must bear
Wave on teaser

In bouts of kisses and pecks
Hugging loosely, they slowly part
Her knight is gone
The passion of yester-night suns her body
Radiating sparks which glows her fair skin
She becomes moody, missing her knight
She could not hold it anymore
Tears of longing dropped from her cloudy eyes
Raining down her cheeks and blessing her chin
Seeking the warmth and closure of his armour
Wondering if he was having succour
With his other daisies

At long last he came to her again
He must have been spent
He strode slowly on his stallion
Covering her this time whole-heartily
Their hugs were thunder-clapping
Her smiles the full moon
Her eyes the sparkling stars

Her knight is here, everything else stands still
Night, the lover of the universe
The dark teaser

Cuss Words

Before you strike that blow
That chokes my bosom
Strike a note my sex is infirm
Being nativity clocked our soul and binds us mates
From your rib, I take your breath I breathe

Before you throw that punch
That punch that staggers my affection
Brood for a moment my heart is fragile
My body is as soft as my walls
It slips with your fluid my ribs cannot poise apart

Your fiery sword slits me to moan in malady
Pressure of your hoe blasts to tilting burns
It blinds like a bristle bow to my soil
It deafens like deadened cell of brick cells

Do not mash me; you ought to sooth my bones
Pummel me with love not your bow
Feed me with adoration not your arrow
To nativity genes are strung
My ego as fragile as an egg

My mind feigns fierceness; it dabbles on beehives
Afore you embed shaft of nectars in your tongue
Sieve from crystal wisdom my psyche strewn supreme
The hourglass of time is submissive to my sex

Before you ruffle my pride
Frame it bruised like the baboon's anus
Exposed, raw, and red at alert
My body is as rocked as my sword

FLAMING HEARTBEATS

If your walls can give it sweet softness
Nurture its succulence would humble my hardened fury
Do not harsh my hatch, your power can reborn me
Smooch me with your roses not your spikes

Feed me with your love not your loathes
Holey, I am caged in these splits of splitters
Splattering my stance, my stalks they stall
Stunt they start, of weakening my roots

Let us wish our love a honey horny
From it bitterness we sap sweetness on aftertastes
Let us wish our love tree-hill frenzy
From stems its climax spews on flowery beds

Our love will make branches
As forever my flower looms
Sighs my Gardner tends me well
When our love withers with care
Our love would sane ages

Our love will make greens
Its forestation evergreen
It would be famed in aftermath grease
Forever my ego would be preserved green
As our love stuns for ages

Feast of Love

Of our love in admiration
The moon bows
From the clouds
It is a feast for our love

The stars dance to our devotion
The clouds twine with the stars
To bring glitters to our hearts
In commitment to urge our love

The sun lingers-on on earth
A glimmer of hope for our love
The meddling rain strays to our path
To moisten our vow

The dews cascade at dawn
Its fresh locks a seal to our bond
Until this day, every day is a feast of our love

Ladies' Night

If you hold me back,
I will be broken
I cannot get a grip on myself
Every moment you break free
I trail your wake to catch your thrill

Let me put your back against the door
And spread your arms across the wall
This night I cannot stop myself
My stiches are itchy naughty
So come all over me

Let us grind as I tickle your pickle
Let your baby's trickles sigh of love
Getting it to play is grand don't delay
I cannot break from you
Your thighs are a perfect holder

Baby hold on to this dance
Let us dance all night long
As we sip wine until the moon squirts
We will have this party all to ourselves

Slowly, let us twist and turn to a toast
On a landing sprawl
Grab me to your bulging chest
Break to the ground with me
The earth will not fall

The jukebox tunes on to our desire
No contours should be left untouched
As our sexual aura rent the air to a blast

This night we cannot stop ourselves
Our cries must raise the roof

Desert Of Longing

Between her thighs I begged to be reborn
The richness my loins have waited ten thousand years
A love I thought would never be fondled
Rolls row and bells on bed of roses
And alight in arrays of candlelight

Between her bosoms I begged to be sated
Day and night I soften my dreams in ice and in cold
Her unyielding smiles lay warm in my soul
But her eyes kept lit and wanton in my mind
My tongue raced feverishly for her lips
But her soul never savoured my words

Within your parted lips I begged to breathe
This night you chose to bear your sculpted glands
I shall drink to fill my airless lungs
I will suck off your lasting juice
I shall wean off your breath of life
To heal this desert of yearning

Torch of Love

With my torch of love
I have roamed the globe
In search of perfect words
To celebrate a blessed joy

With a sigh of ease I realized
In a month God reserved
To form Angels
The lyrics will not take shape

She is a polished verse
Her eyes nourishing
Like the depth of blue waters
From the purest fountain her

Laughter cascades down living spring
Her smiles delectable as fresh roses
Her voice a jailbreak nightingale
Freed to mesmerize our solitary ears

I have memorized her heart of gold
I look no further for a precious stone
Dazed my mind lingers
At her threshold of love

My Love

You are the Amen to my prayers
The testimony of my tests
I thirst to taste
You filled my lips with taste
All my prayers I am yet to thunder
Already my alleluia vibrates from yonder
On grace and grease I ponder
My melody of praise will not be tender
The salvation of my feet dances of wonder
My voice is a clapper of your state
My joy is a limitless wanderer
I hunger to hang
You filled my throat with your tinder
My world is lighter
Because you're my soul lifter
You make all my worries shiver
I will always be your name appraiser
I am your gospel lover
Your words make my heart younger
Forever be my sole minder

Apple in Sodom

I decided to stay home today
Would call in sick at work
I felt guilty for scarcely being home
I want to make up for lost times
He's unease
His face devoid of emotions

Styling every seductive pose
To steer his straying stares
Tried out wardrobe of sultry outfits
To rekindle his passion with burning stares
His mind and body remained chaffed
I've screwed up way out of line
I dashed out only for some minutes

I sauntered into the living room
With tons of goodie bags
He was gone from the settee
There's one haven he could be

Unwinding and twisting my waist
Swinging my hips and popping
Top buttons of my dress
I glided towards our nest of roses
I heard soft moans and hard groans
My senses snapped
My breath breaking
My heartbeat quaking
My steps took strides

Behold a banging binge!
Mine forever, until death do us part

Beneath a same blood
That runs through my veins

I reached for the doorknob
My pond palm slid off
It could, I couldn't hold
My knees buckled
My eyes an itchy ocean
I screamed out words
My lips didn't mouth

She's an experienced rider
Atop a sturdy stallion
They twined as Siemens twin
They're so matched
I thought he was merely mad at me
Never imagined I had become so repulsive

I willed myself to move
But my legs rooted on same spot
Alongside strangled satiated screams from both
I let out pained outrageous cries
Two pairs of bewildered faces turned to me
Faces shamed and crestfallen
Muttered nonsense words of pleas
My mind ravaged for reasons
As I sought solace, anywhere
Darkness embraced me

Interlock

Now, rain has interlocked with the earth
Their wetness is second to none
This land is an insatiable lover
Of dews and moist
On overflowing field of lust
Lost to satisfaction
All soils are gently grappling
With grapes of thorns
The circumstances of their love
Tied with a sacred thread
Only a holy trace can untie
And what is made holy is sanctified
This lust of the flesh is a knot of thistles

Falling In Love

My soul is a shade of blindness
I fell in love with a painter
Now my heart is filled with colours

My mind was savagely loose
I fell in love with a screwdriver
Now my thoughts are tightly knot

My lenses are blurring
I fell in love with a photographer
Now my world has become a photo book

I fell in love with boarders
My journeys without bothers
Now knows no boundary

My world is void of the muse
I fell in love with a poet
Now my heart runs on lines

My bosom never knew warmth
I fell in love with a cheerful fire
Now, my body no longer shivers from cold

In My Eyes

In the dove of our love I see you in my eyes
In my mirror of tears I see our weeping joy
In my shiver of fears I calm in steel rivers
I hear you in my voice
I feel your pulse in my heartbeat
Your caresses are tender hearted
I want your kisses on my temple
To radiate like stars in the night

In the dreamy clouds of our love
I smell your presence in my mind
Your bosom grazing my cheeks
Your unshaved jaw pricking my nape
I want to live a beautiful life with you
A life of soft songs and slow dance

How can I love you forever?
In your arms of tender love
Twirl me around your heart
While I taste the lips of your love
Despise not my love of yore
Do not take away my smiles
In ceaseless carelessness
I want to love you forever

Love of Age

Our love has come to an age
Where we listen with our eyes
Talk with our hearts
And love with our lips

The coldness of our bed
Reminds me your warmth
Has strayed far too long
And haunts the bed

My lonely days are assailed
By nights your delicious smell
Robed my nape with loose whispers
As your breathless kisses intoxicate me

When I inhale your nearness
My heart feels tenderly warm
Tonight when your feet crosses the door
All my lonely nights will be over

For your love I live
I drown in the sweetness
Of your lemonade taste
My lime made out of a lemon
I embrace your masculinity
And feel wonderfully coy
The only thought I cherish
Is to grip you tighter in a tender hug

I sleep waiting for the moment
Our love will wake
And our lips will come

Closely soul to soul

28

Sunny Moon

Tonight
The moon is of sun
My love, the moon is of sunny gold
And the faintness of your footsteps
Tells me how further
You are drifting from me
Your scents fade
Leaving marks of how long
You have been gone
Let the light of the stars guide you home
To my arms
To my most enchanting bosom

Boyfriend

Dear errant boyfriend
I cannot fight over you with a fellow damsel
Do you know why?
It's not certain you are the one
I'd hand my palm wine cup or walk down the aisle with
I cannot say if you're the one to crown my tomorrow
The girl I may have clubbed with hoe and fork
Could be the root, stem or flower to the tree of my life
Imagine when he introduces me to his branches
The sister is solidly speechless
Her pupils dilating, flabbergasted
Appraising my features with a look of disgust
Hate radiating from her sweating
Pointing at me, she yells
'Mum, she's the mad lady that broke my arm!'
'And imprinted land encroacher on my cheeks!'
Mum exclaims, 'what!
You're the Mohammed Ali that tied your Champion's belt
Around my daughter's neck and waist
Son, how dare you bring this brutal bruiser to my home
She that caused my child to be hospitalized for weeks
She, that marred her pretty face for any gentleman to call flowery
Over my tool box will my son screw his knot with your
Blunt blurted screw driver
I'll rather he marries Christy Martin'

So hint me darling
What do I do when my would be mate
Hovers over his sister
Murmuring smothering words on how he vowed
To make his sister's assailant pay painfully
Telling her how sorry he is for bringing in

The monster fighter to flood her hurt past
Promising her with passionate dispassion
To cast that beast into deep red coals

Meanwhile, you are elsewhere frolicking
With your other belles
No, thank you dearie
I'm not about to doom my love life before it holy booms!
Despite how strong and sweet your long
Sugar cane is
It's not worth the tooth ache it will give me later
I don't have cash for touch and go
You can always be a case in the show glass
Like freshly baked hot dog
But I would be moved to the art gallery
As an exhibited antiquity
For the criticism of man and a case study for woman

Derided On Delusion

I thought ours was love
That would astound the walls of resistance
A love to make love
And mould our hearts

All I yearned were kisses
To seal the flow of our love
To fade each scar
With searing kisses

With touches of my love
I thought I could lighten your heart for my soul
My tongue traced your hurt
Down to the bosom

I thought I could liken
Your passion to my heart
To sate each lust with the soothing moist
Of my loving tongue

But I got kissed with a cold smile
Cooling my heats for you
My love has been submerged in coal
Lost in the mines of gold

My Lantern Girl

My lantern girl
You are the light to my goal
The spring of my showers
You are the glow of my tan line

My lantern girl
You illuminate my burdens
Your smile towers
The weight of my dark scowl

My lantern girl
You made me a god
I will gloat to the deities
You're the goddess that
Confessed my light o' love

My lantern girl
You are a beautiful culture of nature
The call of my river floating
The calmer of my wilful turmoil

Trickles of Lightening

Dawn grumbling, dews stuttering
Stutter, stutter, her heart fluttering
Sleep summing its sources, swaying
On the mind, slouching like a sloth

She peeked at the shutters, shutting her sights
Snuggling deeper, deeper into her cocoon
Crooning, humming with whispering air
The oily crows of morning Africa, chirping chips

To the beautiful dawn, dawn washed in splendour's tray
She burrowed, shrink-wrapped in aching dreams
Itching, sneaking into the ecstasy of yester bliss
Lonesome, awesome wholesome night

They were stripped off shrubbery straws
Trampling bare-footed on mowed lawns
Softening and moaning on rose's bed
Paw on the pompom pups

The hummingbird perched, with promises of crinkling pecks
Cuddled suckled the nectar pop pores
Pump prowl, he tickled her fancy
Hush, hush he tackled her fantasy
Crawling on his currency, shush! Shush!!
He flattered her tendency
She tingled to take him to her condo pond
He was hot, hot ready to rock a tumble
Pop, pop the raying sun dragged, scathing hands heated

Scorching her senses to double over
Filtering through her limbs, sapped the flaming infatuation

It ruffled her senses, and her eyes slithered
Sleepy-eyed, she peaked at reality

Stutter; stutter it was just a dream
Some flights are best not boarded
When sorely soured
It can leave the heart throbbing numbs
War against emotions is saggy sour

The hands of dreams can be waged
Outside she stood thrilled, the sun shiny
Her mood gloomy all of a sudden
She did not see it coming,
It cascaded down all sides

Dusting the dry leaves, she inhaled the pure aroma
The scent of raw earth, greased with massive aura
The rain trickles, the dream bust reality
It was a culmination of organic hydrophilic

Omena

Omena
You are the spring that surges through my thoughts
You are the bowl of my contentment
Believe me, Omena it is not a concoction

Omena
You are my prime love
No one mines my love
Safe the scent from your flowery hands

Omena
Your tender kisses are lifts for my soul
They soften my hard ends
They smooth my rough edges
With you my mind heals of ills
My soul eases off hisses

Omena
I am a whisperer of your tender kisses
You are my pumpkin leaves
You pump blood to my veins
Do not leave me halfway to our love
Please do not take leave of our love

Omena
You are the fate of my love
The face of my mind
The faith of my thoughts
Believe me, Omena you calm my storm

Omena
You make my soul

You mine my heart
Believe me and mind my love

Omena
Let me encrypt my name on your bosom
Let me crest your being with my smiles
Please Omena never say ever
Never say ever
My heart has subscribed to the cable of your love

Omena
You are the symbol of my love
The air my lungs long for
The tone my body tunes for
Believe me, Omena your tunic is tonic
That has cloaked my soul in sweet love

Blind Radar

Once again
I stand at the path of loneliness
Staring hard at the vagueness

Of my journey on trials
Trying to find at which turn
I always follow the blind radar

On the foot void of imprints
I creep on walking
To find love again

How I will tread this path
Leaves me rooted
To the spot of my seclusion

Righting the Soul

Shattered Spring

My heart is dripping tears
My eyes crying blood
Send her heart to the sun
Fuel it with solar power
Open her eyes to the silver sky
Let pure heavens wash away her bitter tears

Bear her mind to a galaxy of stars
Let it crystal shine and sparkle like diamonds
Like the finest polished sacred ornament
Deep her feet in the soil
Root them in earth's soft socks

Clothe her with the forest
To make her forever green
Crown her head with a garden
And she, cultured, a cultivated beauty
Oh, horticulturist!
Hold her tender adinfinitu adinfinitu
Sunning and watering in nature's essence

Enclose African violet in Acropolis
Amma nature babbay-baby atrabilarian
Play the paean, let her fox-trot
Let her spring on prancing feet
But the thorns, the thorns she was oblivious

It pricked her soul; it shed her dignity attire
Send her heart to the goldsmith
Let him refine her fading glint
She is no repack, but a new brand
Begin the search, comb the earth

When finally you find that perfect lavender
Be nice to show the perfect bud
So she could epitomize the perfect perfume
To rebrand her imperfect weal
Palomar asked why the weed
Pollinates the nursery plants
Why do thorns have to grow amidst roses?
Why does its steel sharp tit protrude the fragile buds?
In the sanctuary of Amma nature
Laid she her drenched mind
Amma nature absorb in thunderous solace
In racking sobs, dab her eyes in love sanctified
My heart is dripping tears adinfinitu
My eyes crying blood adinfinitu
Amma nature babbay-baby atrabilarian

Kid Gloves

She's fourteen
Heavy for a boy of sixteen
Both of same grades
She has broken the news to her parents
And stunned to why her dear mother
Would weep to such joyous news

To conceive is a beautiful act
To be celebrated
With loud congrats

But little did she know
The hardship that sprawls
Ahead of her fruitful bump

Her mother is a petty trader
The father treats rubber with heat
Her baby Papa's father, a hopeless drunk
And his mum, a sweeper of the highway

She springs round the neighbourhood
Calling out greetings to foes and friends
Giving no hoot to the sarcastic words
Hurled at her by passers-by

Let them wag their snake's tongue all they would
She's a soon to be mother hen
Hatching her chick is all that matters
Nothing else does

With so much love and tenderness,
She pats her now bulging stomach

With smiles as bright as the moon
And shiny as the star

With her expulsion from school
Her darling Baby Daddy would drop out too
He would secure a job as a messenger
While she hawks oranges
With their earnings, they will feed
And take care of their baby
Yes, they'll be fine they feel

Everything will be alright
Having a baby is what matters
It's treasurable silver and gold
Their baby will birth diamonds

Seek and Hide

Gone were the days
We played hide and seek
We hid to be sought
We could take cover at
The back of doors
Under tables and chairs
Beneath shelves and blankets
Behind the staircase and
Our parent's Volkswagen

Nowadays
The jet teenage boys and girls
Play the game of seek and hide
Their hide nooks would be
The confines of a booked or
Checked in guest room
Passenger and back seats
Of a stranger's Rolls-Royce Wraith
Thick bushes and knowledge centres
Construction sites and duty posts
Bar clubs and water pools

In our days
Before the cock crew in the evening
We'd be bathed with water, seated
And awaiting dinner
But they, are getting ready to
Eat the streets credibility
And dare not to return
Until the morning cock crows
Already bathed and towel dried
With the heat of the night

They act as though
They were never fed with the juices
From their mother's coconut cups
As if they sucked the liquid juices
Of cocks from birth

Be warned
Playing off the sidewalks
On busy streets and roads
Can get you knocked down
By a reckless rider on high speed
You will be cleared and scarred
With so much open wounds
This may render you handicapped

The doors of your homes
Are always opened for you all to go in
Be it under key and locked
I'm sure the keys are stationed
Where you can reach them
I humbly beseech you to desist from
Aimlessly trespassing
Street to back, back to street

It doesn't count if you have
Been served breakfast of
Tea made with a full jug of water
One tea bag and a sachet of milk
One cube of sugar and
Five tablets of biscuit
Or you feel you eat too much pounded yam
With goat meat and bitter leaf soup
Gulped down with orange juice

You want to get on the road
And eat out from
A Chinese restaurant on the bill of a bidder
Severed barbecue chicken
Chips and champagne

Stop hurting your fine feathers and tails
Hide and seek is innocent fun gathering
Seek and hide is sniggering fun
It's a wrecking ball
Rocks and rolls you to rot

Defiled Altar

Somewhere someday and now
A girl child offers herself to a
Deceased husband's brother or male relation
For the sake of tradition
If she returns the bride price
To avoid the demeaning pollution
She is deemed a loose woman
And her right to choice sneered at

The flower is more than a society's norm
She is more than a community's values
She is more than a clan's ego
The flower deserves to preserve her pride in a vase
Without conditions and restrictions,
A girl child reserves the right to maintain
An unbreakable relationship with her pollinations
Some laws are made for wrong reasons
The Girl Child needs protective laws
Womanhood is dignified and sacred
It should not be shredded by subjugating traditions

Little Lamb

As I walked along a busy street,
My gaze trailed a baby
Strapped to the mother's back
Struggling to break free
Hands and legs flaring
Making loud shrieking sounds
All in chase to unbuckle

In the recess of my mind
I cajoled the baby
Hold on little lamb
Little one, don't be in a haste
To touch your feet on thorny thresholds
Tarry for however long
Cheer in every second you're carried
Bask in the moments

For a time will come
You shall pave your own paths
Hardly will anyone be there
To hoist you a lather
Not your brother, sister, Pa
Not even your own Ma
Samaritans are diamond and gold

The world is a waterspout
Barely can one seek splendour
Betrayal a scorpion's sting
Deceit circulate like the venom of a cobra
Suspense pent up like a python
Squeezing life out of a human body
Treason as if a million battalion

Has opened incessant fire
On a one-man army
The love is beetle-browed

In time the baby calmed
Wound chubby legs on mother's hip
And clasp arms round neck like a pendant
Yes, that's it baby
Hold on to it all, savour it
For soon the remains of it
Will be as little as a grain of corn

I got back to my shack, news awaited
A neighbour has put to bed, a premature baby
With a hand plastered to my forehead
I pondered what had prompt this early arrival
Little one, what has forced you into this world?
Those relished nutritious fluid from
Your mother's breast made you believe
The world is of milk and honey?
You should have formed a while longer
How did your frail body take in the gush of cold?
I lit thousands of embers to keep you warm
In this hurricane habitat of ours

Ode to Mammary Glands

My tender breasts tend my babies
From cradle to king-size
Mildly they suckle
Possessively they kindle
And all I do is bear tenderly
Caressing their cheeks
I surrender my bosom
Tendering all my life
On plains where blooms flourish
My members flap with pride
I wear my nudity with decency
My busts no longer hold this world in firm delight
My nectar shrivels to earth with fulfilment
And nature flags it down with grace
For I bloom for its succour
And wane for its pleasure

Hourglass

They would not relent
Until every bit of her dignity is shred
If she had lain bare to their biddings
Her body would have been smeared
With different shades of colour
Blue, black, and no red
She would have come out in rainbow

If she had done it
She would not be standing tall
Head held high, walking like the peacock
Rather her buttocks turned up
For preying by the Chimpanzees
With series of furious whippings
Legs and thighs clubbed in stigma

She wouldn't pine
For the loss of half shades
If she did
She would be regretting
The formative years of her bloom

The pretty ones remained humble
The ugly personified paraded pride
She was hard driven by them
Neither to ruins nor dishonour
Rather, tending onward
Ground breaker and earth mover

They succeeded not in marring
But making her an unearthing element
Kiting in the air, skating on mountains

Bending fire, breaking waters
Mining coals, drilling soils
Seasonally sowing seeds
Weeding weeds with bulldozers
Dying parasitic cells
Swelling with peaceful pride
Of her blooming fields
She doused her face
With dew drops from the sky
Glossed her lips with the rising sun
Winking impishly at the heavens
She hummed, *gracias* for manipulating them
To make her

Rebranding Her Childhood

When she was so heavy with me
I must have weighed
Nine coconuts in her wee basket
Cuddled in her hearth warmly
Wrapped with protective layers
And cells of scented mire and gold

At the auspicious season
She pushed me forth and
Smiled down at my clean limbs
Wealthy with wisdom
That I can run the race of life
The tricky lane of a lone race

She cradled me to her bosom
And sang the lyrics of my birth
Toeing the crawls of my growth
Growing she held me firmly
By my wrist and crossed roads
When blows of life shook my storey
Threatening to erase my bloom
She hugged me to the fortitude of her tattered gown

When the whips of life lashed out
Tirelessly at my hunched back
Bent from the burden of life's tests
She gave me her shoulders
To weep off my pains
And her dolphin ears whenever
I buzzed out my heartaches
Her bosom absorbed my pains

When she was young, full of life
I pampered her
Wore perfumed talc on her lush face
She licked it off her pout lips
Babbling tasty and sweet and softly
I massaged her ample ankles with mild oil

When she was staggering
I gave her my shoulders
To crawl up from her blanket
When she was too soft to carry on
I knew her nappy eyes needed to dream
I raised her high above my tummy top
And laid for her the finest fluffy furs
For a luxurious siesta

With tender-hearted care
I spoon-fed her milky pap
With lovingly sweetness
I lifted her high up to my bosom
With the greatest love
I held and twirled her round the room
With utmost love I breathed in
The baby fragrance of her clothes
And bathed her with lavender-scented water
Garnished with lilac Jasmine flowers
Her pyjamas so dry and soft like diapers
I sing her a lullaby, luring her to slumber

With the wake of the morning
I felt warm eyes scrutinizing my face
My eyes grumbled open
And I heard an absurd question
'Who are you?' from her
Forewarned by the doctors

My mind jerkily registered
That her memory has lapsed
I told her I am her nanny
She nodded agreeably
And stretched her warm hands
Firmly I placed mine on them
It is so plum and lush

Trusting and comfortable
She held me in a warm gaze
I clasped hers with the perch of a butterfly
Leading her into the dining set
Time to cook some cereals and broth
She is my baby to cherish
To guide through the deep waters of life
To nurture to health and life

You Did Not Win

Her distraught children looked on
As she writhed on with untold pains
Each spasm drilled her being
For every ragged breath she drew
They prayed it be her last
Oh! In such agonizing time
Is this what it is to be of grey age?

That firm stomach that once enclosed embryos
Brought forth babies
Is now a withered bread fruit
Those succulent breasts
That supplied nourishment when suckled
Are now sapped of sweet liquid
And look like wet padded dried pawpaw leaves

The face which encased contentment
Budding joy of motherhood
When gazed upon by her suckling babes
And seemed a heavenly humble abode
Is now a beaten earth
Oh life! By and by
Beautiful and sweet

Beguiling and sorrowful
Oh sweet mother!
Yet, even in this silence
She looks so enthralled, peaceful
Ready to traverse the world beyond
And just like sleep steals consciousness

The searing cold of death came enveloping

With groping hands that snatched her
Yes, the best of sleep has come
Sweetest of rest has come
From a distance
The loud wails of the children is heard

Mother

On your soil these buds found not a thorn
On your earth our fountain flows without a price
On that bed with soft roses you bore hard
On this auspicious day of nature's harvest
You should hold this planet hostage

You are nature herself
A stem of countless branches
For a Ship a She
For a Nation a She
And Justice a She blinded to gender

Beloved shepherd
We will adorn your fingers with worship
While we coo a corsage on your wrist
Anointing have we savoured
When we touch our heads to your fore

On my thighs where I dedicate your feet
Will I woo it weaknesses
With my humble strength
Ace with ointment
In this room I've left cosy

Warmed with tallow candle
Scented with finely burnt kernel
This is my service to you
For your service hole delicately spew me forth
Crying and sucking

Hale and hearty
Lying and crawling

Standing and walking
Just as you womb me
I will always keep you home

Affectionate

A mother's affection is not affectation
At the stool of birthing nations
She makes heaven counsellor
A firm decider of her faith
To live or not to breathe

Her cries are between anguish and joy
At the stables of life and death
She makes war with infelicity
And comes out victorious
With sprouting seedlings

A mother's mothering is eternal
Her duty everlasting
A mother never stops giving suckle
She never retires from nursing

She is that evergreen tree
That never loses its leaves
Its stems are a covenant
That her heart is a covetous spirit
Its marks on earth are infinite

62